# Take Up Space



J. Olympus Fisher

BookLeaf Publishing

Presentation by *BookLeaf Publishing*

Web: www.bookleafpub.com

E-mail: info@bookleafpub.com

ISBN: 9789357213585

First edition 2023

# DEDICATION

This book is dedicated to my spouse, who continues to remind me, every day, that I am capable of achieving my dreams.

# ACKNOWLEDGEMENT

Thank you to the therapists who supported me through some of the scariest times of my life and believed in me when I couldn't believe in myself.

Thank you to the friends who have  held space for me to cry or vent about what I was experiencing and who have allowed me to share my poetry with them.

And thank you to my TikTok family, who has shown me, over and over, that I deserve love and gentleness and kindness, in ways the my biological family never did.

# PREFACE

Written words have helped me survive every traumatic experience in my life. In writing, is one of the only places that I have always felt truly free to just…take up space.

These poems detail some of the most painful moments of my life and may be triggering for some readers. But these poems are part of my healing journey and if you're on that journey too, my hope is that these poems will serve as reminder of hope.

Healing is painful. But it is possible. And the load feels lighter when we don't take the journey alone.

# Be Kind

Maybe beating yourself up
For letting yourself down
Isn't the answer
And maybe you should consider
Hear me out
Just consider
Being kind to yourself
You're not defective or ruined
You're simply just human
And you're deeply prone to flaw
Just like any human is
So do you really think
That being mean
Is gonna get you anywhere
You've shown kindness to rapists
Abusers
And liars
And people who didn't care
About what they did to you
So why do you refuse
To show yourself a little kindness too
You think there's something so special
About you
That basic human decency doesn't apply to you
But you're not wrong

You're not that special
No one is
You're not a bad person
But you've seen some bad things
And those things that you've seen
Are like poison to your mind
But the antidote is kindness
And you're the only one who can give it
You were a child
And all you knew was all you know
So why do you think
You should've known better
Stop punishing yourself
And realize
You're human
You're broken and healing
All at the same time
And maybe it wouldn't be so hard
If you would just be a little kind

Not Okay
When I was just a little girl
My brain was forced to keep me safe
So it built these walls up in my mind
To protect me from the pain
Those walls cage monsters
That have been hungry for so long
Now that they're under attack
The walls aren't holding strong

And those monsters are hungry
After years of starvation
They've started destroying
With no hesitation
I'm scared and alone
And I'm lost in this space
And I need someone to see
That I'm not okay
I'll tell you I'm fine
As they claw through my soul
Because I'll be an inconvenience
If I lose control
You can't see what's happening
There's no blood and no bruise
So all these things that I'm feeling
Are probably just an excuse
'Cause I can't prove what I'm saying
I can't make you believe
So it's just for attention
Making everything about me
I don't have the words
To say that I need help
'Cause I'm just being dramatic
I should keep it to myself
But these monsters will kill me
If I don't let them out
I can't reach the door
And my voice won't let me shout
I have so much to say

But don’t want to burden with my needs
And the things I could tell you
You may not even believe
I’m trying hard to fight them
But these monsters are screaming
They’re strong and they’re loud
And it feels like I’m dying
I’m really not okay
But I can’t say that out loud
And I’m begging for help
Without making a sound
I need someone to hear me
Screaming from within
Because these monsters want to kill me
And I’m scared they’re gonna win

# Hold Me

He held me so tight
Wrapped me in his strong arms
And I felt safe with my daddy
Free from any harm
In his arms I felt special
Protected from the whole world
Because being held in his arms
I was his sweet baby girl
Wrapped up in our blanket
His hands tended to wander
Arising sensations in my body
Filling me with fear and wonder
I felt comfort when he held me
Reminded me I was not alone
He was my foundation
To remind me I was home
He showed me how to love
And how to endure pain
He confused the taste of affection
With the burden of shame

So now comfort is confusing
And safe connection isn't real
Love's a risk I dare not take
'Cause I can't handle how it feels

I asked for the attention
And I liked the way it felt
So maybe I should just learn to stomach
The shame of being held
My body's screaming out for warmth
My heart is begging to be soothed
But I can't feel the touched of kindness
Without the shame of being used

Please hold me, I'm desperate
For the warmth of loving touch
But oh my god, don't touch me
I don't want to feel that loved
I'm craving attention
For someone to just see me
But I'm so ashamed of my wants
And terrified of my needs
I need to be held
I need to know that I'm safe
But safety and connection
Can't exist in the same space

# Winner

"I know that you're not
That's why I showed up
You're gonna realize I'm right
You'll never be enough
Your followers hate you
That support is a lie
They'd all celebrate the loss
If you'd go ahead and just die"

Stop it, stop talking
Get out of my head
Maybe you're right
And I should just be dead
I'm so tired of hurting
I just want it to stop
I've fought for so long
And I think Ive gotten lost

"You are lost, you're stuck
You'll never get out
You're too weak to fight me
Time to throw in the towel
You won't survive this one
Should you choose to fight

Go ahead and just quit
No one will care if you die"

It's not true, you're lying
I think I'm gonna be sick
I have so much life left to live
But I can't handle all this
Why are you yelling
Why won't you let me go
Things will get better
Gotta hold onto hope

"You don't get it do you
You'll never get better
Because no matter what you do
You'll always be a loser
You're a waste of space, trash
And your life is a joke
Your existence will fade
Just like a post fire smoke"

Shut up! Shut up!
I don't want to die
I have so much left to say
I want to feel more alive
Stop lying to me
You're not going to win
You won't make me stop
I'll fight you again and again

“You think you’re that strong, huh
You don’t realize you’re weak
You’ll break and you’ll shatter
And I’ll have a feast
I’ve waited you out before
So it’s just like old times
Let me know when you’re ready
To give me your life”

I’ll never be ready
I’ll never give up
I’ll keep fighting and proving
That I am enough
I deserve to live
And I deserve to find peace
I’ll prove that I’m worthy
Of being believed

“And there it is right there
I don’t even have to do the work myself
I’ll just wait until you’re trapped
Inside your “proving your worth” shell
The pain will sit on your skin
And burn through to your soul
And you’ll cry out to me
When you’ve finally lost control”

You’re twisting my words
I’m begging leave me alone

I’m weak and I’m tired
And I just want to go home
I want the fighting to end
And I don’t want to let you win
But I’m afraid that if I beat you
I’ll be a winner once again

# I'm Not Me

Sometimes it feels
Like I'm not really me
I can't explain it in words
Because I know it sounds crazy
I live in this body
But I don't know who I am
Like I'm lost in my head
How can I make you understand
I remember everything
But I forget everything else
I'm here enough to function
But I'm locked inside a shell
Because I exist inside my brain
But that's the only place I am
Because every place I've ever gone
I wear the mask I need for them
As a child I was punished
For simply existing how I was
So my brain created an image
Who was more deserving of love
I became convenient
And distanced me from the truth
Because existing just as me
Would've shown off too much proof
So I'm a completely different person

But at least that person's safe
I don't remember what she said
But she had on the right face
I can feel everything, always
While also feeling nothing
I'm floating off in space
Trying to hold on to something
I know that I'm existing
Because I know my body's real
But I don't know how to let my body
And my brain connect to feel
I can read a room in seconds
And in an instant, change my face
Because my brain's top priority
Is making sure I'm safe
It's not a choice I ever made
To become me and she and her
To separate myself from the reality
It's just how my brain works
If you don't like the person who I am
It's really no big deal
You can just choose another
From my personality wheel
It's both a gift and curse
To be such a chameleon
I learned how to change my colors
So I'd always fit right in
But which face belongs on mine
Which color's truly me

How do I create a whole person
From each fragmented piece
I'm consistently inconsistent
I'm flakey and confused
Was that fake, was that real
Am I even telling the truth
I've never had a strong foundation
Of knowing who I am
And I don't have an answer
When asked about my plans
I'm not the same person right now
As who I was yesterday
And who I'll be tomorrow
Is a question for another day
Maybe I'm just indecisive
And need to learn to make a choice
But my brain can't even conceptualize
How to become just one voice
It's like I'm watching my own body
Exist throughout this life
And I'm starting to panic
The more that I realize
I have no clue who I am
I don't know which me is me
Or how to tell you in a way
That you'll even believe
Because I've masqueraded in this body
For several decades now
I locked myself inside for safety

And now I can't get out
My brain does what it needs
To keep me safe and protected
But being someone else all the time
Has left my soul exhausted
They tell me just to trust my heart
And I'll find the answers in myself
But I don't know what that means
And I think I need some help
How do I trust which me is me
How do I know which me I am
'Cause I have all these personalities
But I'm not any of them
Maybe I really am crazy
And I'm just losing my mind
But if I put on the right face
I can smile and say I'm fine

# Fragments of my Soul

It's like there's a constant battle
Going on inside my brain
Between who I really am
And the things I do and say
We can't control our thoughts
And can't control what we feel
I can control my behaviors
But I'm not always sure what's real
Sometimes I see me speaking
But I'm not really present
I promise it's not on purpose
I just feel so distant
I want to stay here in this moment
But I don't really know how
To let myself call the shots
I'd have to get myself out
Like I can see myself living
A life that belongs to me
But the person existing
Is just a fragment of a piece
I don't remember things I've said
Or what I might've done
Because inside my mind, I'm hiding
It's safer there alone
Sometimes I'm outgoing

And sometimes I'm shy
Both times I'm a person
That I don't recognize
"Get it together"
I'm often telling myself
But myself doesn't listen
And myself often yells
Eventually the world will notice
What I already do
That I'm not a real person
And I've been hiding the truth
Because what is the truth
And who am I as a person
Am I lying for attention
Maybe forgetting on purpose
The whole concept of time
Feels like it's all just made up
Because time's not a thing
I can reach out and touch
Like I know the day happened
Because the clock told me so
And I'm still living, still breathing
But I'm not really home
The autopilot takes over
And life just goes on
I do what I have to do
But behind these eyes, I'm gone
I've lived thirty plus years
Trying to figure out how to be

Because everything I had learned
Said I couldn't be me
Some days are confusing
It's just that nothing feels right
And there's not really a reason
I just don't want to be alive
Because nothing make sense
And I'm scared of who I might be
If I crack open the shell
And set myself free
But some days are amazing
And I feel so alive
Like on those days I forget
The things I've survived
I wish I could be the same person
All of the time
And be consistently consistent
Down to the things that I like
Am I the me who is kind
Who loves with her whole heart
Or am I the me full of anger
Who tears strangers apart
Am I actually outgoing
Do I really need all those friends
Or am I shy and alone
Do I like existing in my head
Am I really a perfectionist
Who must have everything done right
Or am I okay with a mistake or two

If that's what it takes to survive
All these voices in my head
Are all the fragments of my soul
That's why it's so loud in here
They're all fighting for control

# I Can't Speak

The peace I built for myself
Doesn't grow too heavy

It doesn't cave in on itself
Or sag at the edges

It holds itself up strong and true
Just the way I built it
All those years ago

It grew out of quiet nights
And whispered prayers
Of my mother before she went to sleep

Fortified by wise teachings of the Word
Paired with faith and given trials that tested the endurance

Of a peace often searched for
But a feeling never bought

That I built for myself
And for which more than a few times
Has a battle been fought.The only place I can speak

Is in stanzas and lines
Because the words that I say
Don't feel like mine
Because it's not safe
To say these things out loud
So when I put words on paper
It all comes pouring out
My fears and my hopes
My desperation to be seen
I've been screaming out for so long
For someone to believe
But maybe it's me
Who needs to set myself free
I can say those words
But what does that even mean
I'm trapped in my own brain
And it's lonely in here
But I can't get past
The weight of the fear
So maybe I'll just keep speaking
The only way I know how
And maybe one day
I'll speak it all out loud

# I’m Here

I’m shaking
Where am I
I’m here
No I’m not
What’s happening
I’m empty
But I’m full
I feel like I’m gonna puke
I can’t do this
I’m losing my mind
I’m drowning
And my body is tired
I can’t keep on fighting
Can anyone help me
Maybe toss me a lifesaver
Before my body gives up
I can’t do this
I’m torn
I’m tired of trying
If I had just been better
Then I wouldn’t be dying
No, stop lying
I have to keep fighting
But I can’t do this
I’m losing it

My sanity's slipping
I don't know what's happening
I'm here
No I'm not

# You're Fine

"Stop crying, you're fine
Why can't you just move on
You survived alright
And it made you so strong
You're just being dramatic
It wasn't really that bad
It's your own crazy thoughts
That're making you sad"

I was there when it happened
I remember what he did
But I knew nothing else
Because I was just a little kid
It's not just crazy thoughts
What happened was real
And for 30 some years
I've been too scared to feel

"Too scared to feel?
You're making that up
Your childhood was nothing
But kindness and love
You were a terrible child
Your mom did what she could
But she couldn't do much

‘Cause you just weren’t good”

There’s no such thing as bad children
Just kids with unmet needs
I was desperate for safety
And was begging to be seen
Maybe she loved me as best she could
But it was never enough
Because anything she ever gave me
Was conditional love

“You’re such a spoiled brat
When will you grow up
Bad things happen sometimes
And life is just tough
No one wants to listen
To all your made up lies
And no one even believes
Any of your fake cries”

Life for sure isn’t easy
I know that so well
I tried pretending I was fine
But that facade fell
This pain is relentless
And I’m falling apart
Because decades of denial
Takes a toll on the heart

# The Haze is Lifting

I feel like I'm waking up
For the very first time
And I'm realizing the things I've seen
Aren't what I pretended them to be
The games that we played
And the love that we shared
The past is unraveling
And I'm seeing it all for what it really was

Play dates and parties
And quality time with my dad
Were really secrets and shame
But I thought I was special
Because he loved me
But the games that we played
Weren't games at all
They were horrific abuse
That erased my innocence

The love and support
Of my protective mom
Was really manipulation
And control
And I only deserved that love and support
If I earned it

So when I was bad
I deserved the pain too

I've been brainwashed and blinded
And lost in the haze for long
But the haze is lifting
And my eyes are seeing the truth
For the very first time
And it's just as terrifying
As it is liberating

# Invisible

Healing isn't linear
Yeah, I know
But damnit I'm tired
And this shit is fucking hard
It's a roller coaster
Up and down
Up and down
I do okay for a little while
And then suddenly I'm not
But I convince myself if I could do better
And be better
I'd feel better
But I'm not better
The roller coaster makes me sick
Healing is not linear
I'm trying to remember
But when I'm frozen in the panic
I feel like a failure
I'm so tired
The thoughts don't stop
The memories never end
I can't do this
I don't want to feel it
I feel guilty
And weak

And insecure
And overwhelmed
And angry
God, I'm so angry
So fucking angry
How did no one ever notice
How did no one ever know
No one ever saw anything
Because I'm invisible
I always have been
And as long as I do and say the right things
No one asks any questions
Smile and nod
And don't let anyone know
What's really going on
Because they won't understand
And I'll just make waves
It's easier to just smile and nod
It's safer to just follow along
Because I don't want to give anyone
The space to hurt me
And too much vulnerability
Opens a door to comfort
And that requires trust
And the only person I trust anymore
Is me
But I'm unpredictable
And trauma has a mind of its own
And as much as I trust me

I don’t trust my trauma
Sure, my trauma made me strong
But strong isn’t what I needed
I needed safe
I needed to be seen
And heard
And understood
I needed love
And connection
And hope
But instead I got shame
And fear
And lies
And more pain than my brain could process
I needed to be safe
But I was invisible
Because trauma taught me
That I didn’t deserve to be seen
But what if being seen is what I need

# Don’t Drown

I can hear my heart beating
And I can’t catch my breath
I’m gasping
But nothing is coming
I’m drowning
Trying to just keep swimming
But what if I don’t want to
I’m screaming
But no one can hear me
It’s deafening
The voice in my head
Echos I’m failing
And I’ll never make it
But I’m trying
With everything in me
And I’m begging myself to just keep on going
It’s exhausting
My muscles are shaking
And I’m pleading with myself
To just make it to tomorrow
I’m breaking
All the parts of me crumbling
And I keep on remembering
All the times that they hurt me
But I’m healing

And I keep one day hoping
It won't be like this forever
So for now I'll just try
To keep myself from sinking

# What's Real

I can feel hands on my neck
And breath on my skin
And just like that I'm there
Reliving the whole thing again
I'm begging my brain
To just know what is real
But all I can see
Is how painful this feels
My body remembers
Every time I was hurt
And all the shame inside me
Tells me it was deserved
But it wasn't deserved
And that shame isn't mine
So what if I'm honest
And I say I'm not fine
Because I'm not doing fine
And I'm not okay
I know that I will be
But I'm not, today
I'm sick to my stomach
With an ache in soul
From the memories of things
I could never control
I want to forget

And I want to heal
But I’m still here doubting
What’s fake and what’s real

# Get to Know Her

Do you ever look in the mirror
And feel like you're looking into the eyes of stranger
Because I see my face
My smile
My eyes
But it doesn't look like me
Those eyes are hollow and sad
And that smile is struggling to find joy
In even the best parts of life
Because I can't see a way out
My heart is panicked
Almost all of the time
Like it's going to beat right out of my chest
My brain senses danger
And says I'm not safe
But there's no clenched fists or a gun in my face
And it doesn't matter how many times
I remind myself that I'm safe
My brain is certain I'm not
But maybe safety isn't just not dying
And maybe safety includes not being scared
To exist or to just speak
Maybe safety is also feeling secure in the idea of just who I am as a person

He says it'll get better and it won't be like this forever
But his actions never change
So I just stand here wondering if I'm crazy
Because he loves me
And he wouldn't hurt me
But that's what he's doing
He's hurting me
So either he doesn't love me and he's doing this intentionally
Or he needs help to see
The pain that his choices have caused me
Because apparently love isn't supposed to hurt
But love has always hurt
So how the hell was I supposed to know otherwise
Because no one ever told me that I don't deserve to live in constant fear
That every word I speak is going to be wrong
And that every thought I think is going to be irrational
And that every feeling I feel is going to be dramatic

I shouldn't be scared of trusting myself
And yet over and over again
The people I trusted have continually taught me
That I can't and I shouldn't even begin to trust me

So how do I know what to believe
How do I know what's me
And what's him
And what's them
I want to know who I am outside of all of them
All of the people who I've allowed to define me
And all of the people who taught that I couldn't trust me
My mind bought the lies
And I followed them blindly
And I couldn't even see that it wasn't me

If I can't trust myself and the things that I see
The things that I feel and the things that I think
Then who can I trust
If I'm going to let other people define me
Then I'll continue to be lost

I have no clue who I am
And that face in the mirror looks like a complete stranger
But maybe if I take the time to sit down and listen
I can get to know her

# Run-on Sentence

My life is a run-on sentence
And I don't know how to use a period
I try to drop in a comma at least once every few days
So that I'll remember to pause
And breathe
But the next word is always starting
While the last one is still lingering
And the next idea starts dancing
Before the last one is bowing
Have you ever read something
With misplaced punctuation
It becomes much harder to understand

Have I become a run-on sentence
That no one knows how to read

# Could It Be

Could it be
That I'm just scared to feel peace?
Because, really...

I was molded by chaos
By lies and deception
It's really, honestly just surprising
That I became an adult
With even a minimal ability to pretend I can function
But underneath the appearance
Of being able to function
Is a hidden destruction
And self-deprivation
Because I really don't actually believe that I matter...
Oh, well that's a telling realization
Peace is calm
And it feels unsafe
Can someone make that feeling
Make any sense to me?
If what I really want more than anything
Is to simply feel peace

Why am I also consumed by terror the moment I even start to feel something in the realm of happy
These feelings are so intensely confusing
And sometimes I feel like I'm utterly losing
This battle for my very own soul
Could it really be possible that I could reprogram
All of these distorted thoughts inside my head
And really learn how to feel joy that isn't tainted by feeling guilty?

Could it be,
That it's really okay to have needs?
Honestly, just hear me...

Humans have needs
And that doesn't mean that I'm needy
At least
That's what my therapist tells me
And just...
Hmm...
I'm just a bit skeptical
I mean, that sounds good in theory
But is that really true for me?
Okay, let's be real
She's probably right
And what I call neediness

Is literally just me being a human who
desperately just wants to survive
And what if the cure for "neediness"
Is simply getting my needs met
Getting my needs met?
It feels like such a nice concept
I mean, it briefs well
But I seem to execute it poorly
Repetitively
Like, over and over again
I may know what I need, but my voice refuses to
even speak
Because I have no concept or context
Of how to even stand up for me
Can I really just stand up and say, "hey, these are
my needs."
It can't really be that simple
Is it?
But it's so terrifying
Because what if I say what I need and someone
else says I'm lying?
How do I know who's okay to trust
Who will accept my needs and still treat me with
love?
Or am I actually supposed to expect that from
everyone?

Could it be,
That I don't need to feel guilty?
Alright, listen to me...

I made some bad choices
Yeah, that was pretty dumb
But those choices don't mean
That I'm not still a ridiculously amazing and strong and resilient human
Why do I really feel guilty?
Think about that
No, I mean like...
Really think about that
Do I feel guilty
Because I actually think I'm really not worthy
And that I shouldn't expect the same level of human empathy and kindness as everyone else
Because just FYI, self, incase I didn't know
I am and I do
I deserve the same love and compassion
As I'd give my best friend
If they call me crying at 3am
Crying because life once again
Ripped the rug out from underneath them

Could it be,
That I'm not really an inherently bad human being,
Woah, that's heavy...

Because really I was a traumatized child
Who learned a whole host
Of maladaptive coping skills because my brain
Was just trying to keep me alive
During the most traumatic times of my life
And now I've had to spend
My entire adult existence trying to undo the damage
Done by the hands of men
Who never cared if I lived or died
By the hands of grown adults who manipulated my mind
They lied and disguised
And taught me how to hide
All the deepest and darkest and scariest part of my life
But could it really be
That all those disgusting parts of me that I hate to see
Are really just the memories
Of the terrible things that were done to me
I wasn't born wrong
And I didn't deserve what was done
Let me say that again
To make sure I really heard
I didn't deserve what was done to me
None of it
And I don't deserve to feel guilty
For choices I didn't make

And I don't deserve to carry the shame
Or any of the pain
And I am strong
And resilient
And brave
And like a million other amazing things
That my abusers tried to destroy about me

# What’s Wrong With You

You were told
That there was something wrong with you
So you’ve spent your whole life
Trying to fix it
You hated yourself
For everything you tried so hard to change
But what if I told you
There was never anything wrong with you
And that you weren’t a problem
That needed to be fixed
You’ve been traumatized
And horrifically abused
By the hands of people who said they loved you
There was never anything wrong with you
So stop trying to fix yourself
Stop trying to make yourself enough
For everyone around you
And fall in love with the idea
That you are enough
In and of yourself

# I’m You

I don’t want to see you
But I can see you crying
I don’t want to hear you
But I can hear you screaming
I can’t
Because it hurts too much
To remember how much you’ve been through
You aren’t me
I can’t be you
Because if I’m you
Then this is real
And I have to face the reality
That these things that you’ve seen
Completely destroyed me
I can tell your story
But I can’t see me
It’s your story
Not mine
And I’m fine
No, really
I’m fine
I just don’t want to see you
I’m sorry
I know you’re begging to be seen
But I can’t help you

Your pain is too painful
Your pain
It's a part of your story
Oh god
I can't do this
I can't hear you
The weight of the pain
That shakes in your tiny voice
Is crushing
You didn't deserve it
You deserved love
And safety
And kindness
And all the joy in the world
No one listened
No one would see you
No one would hear you
Just like no one saw me
And no one heard me
Because you are me
I'm you
And I have to heal you
If I want to heal me
Your story is mine
And, no
I'm not fine
The weight of the fear
Might eat me alive
And somehow you survived

I’m in awe of your strength
Your resilience and courage
You’re the bravest person I’ve ever seen
Because I’m seeing you
And I see your spirit fighting
Always refusing to give up
Or give in
I wouldn’t even be here now
If it wasn’t for you
But you are me
And I am you
And if I’m going to have compassion for you
That means having compassion for me
And I can’t believe that I deserve it
But you do
And I’m you

# How

I've asked why
So many times
But why isn't really
What I want to know
Because knowing why now
Won't change the past
I think the question is really just how
How do I keep living
And reliving
And reliving
Every painful memory
And still figure out a way
To keep going
To trust me
Like I exist only in memories
How do I feel all the pain
Without letting myself go
Keep up with the house
The dishes
The laundry
It's exhausting
And there's work
And kids
And pets
And friends

Each task requires
A different version of me
Oh and we have to eat dinner
But it's excruciating
The pain in my body
I can feel every memory
And I don't want to get out of bed
Let me stay here and die
It'll eat me alive
They say balance
It's balance
You gotta learn how to balance
But how do I balance
The weight of my past
With the pressure of everything now
Be kind
It takes time
You'll figure it out
And I'm sure that I will
I just don't know how

# Talk About It

I don't want to talk about it
Okay
Maybe I do
But how
The words burn in my throat when I try to speak them
And my mind goes blank
I panic
I'm scared
I can't speak
Because if I speak the unspeakable
You'll never look at me the same
Or maybe I'm more worried
That I will never look at me the same
But we have to talk about it
I have to talk about it
Because it's burning inside of me
Like acid coursing through my veins
Every memory is a dose of poison
And some days it feels like I will die here
When I can feel his hands tighten around my neck
When I can feel their hands against my skin
When I can hear his voice
I can't breathe

My heart races
It’s not real
I am safe
But it was real
And I wasn’t safe
I want to kill the memories
And forget this ever was a part of me
But that means I have to face them
And I think that mean I have to talk about it

# Shut Up and Listen

Listen to me
I'm not going to put it nicely anymore
You are so fucking valuable
You are precious
And priceless
And so damn worthy
Of every good thing
This life has to offer you
You've dismissed it
And denied it
So many damn times
But right now
You need to shut up and listen

You have a strength inside of you
That can be matched by few
You have fought back
Against everything that has tried to kill you
And you're still here
You're still fighting to survive
And you say that's not strength
But if that's not strength
Then you tell me what is

Because strength is standing up
After life has knocked you down
And demanding to survive
Because even at your weakest
Something inside of you knew
That you were worth so much more
Than all the shit that you've been though
You fought like hell
No one else did that for you
Do you see it?

You are a survivor
With the heart of a fighter
The soul of dreamer
And the strength of a warrior
And it's about damn time
That you recognize that about yourself

# The Words

There's a closet in my mind
That I am terrified to open
Because after years and years of negligence
It's started overflowing
The door has started shaking
And the screams are echoing
These words I hold inside me
Are gonna be the thing that kills me
Because nothing else hurts me like the things I don't say
Expect for the things that I say over and over
But only inside my mind
And only to myself
Because I can't let anyone else know
What a scary place it is
Inside my brain
And the amount of pain I can inflict
With the words I don't say
But don't worry
I'm only hurting myself
I just need to put it all away
Locked in that closet
But what do I do
When it starts to give way
And the door starts to break

And all of those unspoken words demand to escape
The words have to be spoken
But I don't know what to say

www.ingramcontent.com/pod-product-compliance
Lightning Source LLC
Chambersburg PA
CBHW051736130826
49812CB00033B/882
*9789357213585*